The KidHaven Science Library

Atoms

by Don Nardo

KidHaven Press, an imprint of Gale Group, Inc.
10911 Technology Place, San Diego, CA 92127

Library of Congress Cataloging-in-Publication Data
Nardo, Don, 1947–
    Atoms / by Don Nardo.
      p. cm. — (Kidhaven science library)
    Summary: Discusses the discovery of atoms and how they work,
nuclear energy and weapons, nuclear radiation and its medical
uses, atomic clocks, and other applications.
    ISBN 0-7377-0942-1 (hardback : alk. paper)
    1. Atoms—Juvenile literature. 2. Nuclear energy—Juvenile litera-
ture. 3. Radioactivity—Juvenile literature. [1. Atoms. 2. Nuclear
energy. 3. Radioactivity.] I. Title. II. Series.
    QC173.16 .N37 2002
    539.7—dc21

    2001002963

Contents

Chapter 1

The Building Blocks of Matter

"**M**atter" is the general name given to the various substances that make up the universe. Stars, planets, and comets in the distant reaches of outer space are composed of matter. So is Earth and everything on it. Mountains, oceans, the air, the soil, buildings, cars, plants, animals, and people—all are made up of matter.

Long ago, people assumed that matter was completely solid. This seemed to make perfect sense. After all, rocks, trees, and people all look and feel solid. However, a few ancient Greek thinkers suggested that matter is not solid. They proposed that all things are made up of tiny particles too small to see with the eye. They called these microscopic building blocks of matter "atoms." Very few people accepted this idea, however. Because no one could see or touch atoms, the common view was that they did not exist.

Jupiter (left) and its moon, Io, are among the many objects made up of matter.

Then, in the nineteenth century, experiments began to show that the Greek thinkers had been right. In the past century and a half, scientists have proven that all matter is made up of atoms. Researchers have shown that numerous kinds of atoms exist. And these various kinds of atoms combine in thousands of different ways. Each combination results in a different and special variety of matter; that is why substances such as water, stone, grass, and human skin are so different from one another.

Extremely Tiny and Numerous

Though the substances that make up stone and human skin are different, their atoms have one thing in common. Like all atoms, they are extremely tiny and numerous. The period at the end of this sentence has enough room to hold many millions of atoms. In fact, 250 million average-size atoms placed side by side would stretch just one inch. Put another way, the number of atoms in a single human body is larger than the number of grains of sand on all the beaches in the world.

Even smaller than the atom itself are its tiny parts. The largest, heaviest part of an atom is its **nucleus**, which rests at its center. The nucleus contains two main kinds of particles. One is called a "**proton**"; the other, a "**neutron**." Because these and other parts of atoms are smaller than atoms themselves, scientists label them "**sub-atomic**" particles.

Another subatomic particle, the **electron**, is much smaller and lighter than a proton or neutron. (In fact, more than 99.9 percent of an atom's weight rests in the nucleus. The electrons make up most of the rest of the weight.) An atom's electrons move around its nucleus, similar to the way Earth and the other planets orbit the sun. Moreover, the electrons orbit very far from the nucleus. Imagine a large-scale model of an atom

One person's body contains more atoms than the grains of sand found on all of Earth's beaches.

in which an ordinary baseball represents the nucleus. The electrons would be tiny grains of sand orbiting more than six miles away! That means that an average atom is made up almost entirely of empty space.

Some subatomic particles carry electrical charges. Electricity is the energy that powers our lights, toasters, televisions, and computers. On a much smaller scale, a proton carries a tiny charge of electricity. That charge is positive. By contrast, an electron carries a negative charge of electricity. The positive and negative charges usually balance, or cancel, each other. So the atom itself usually has no electrical charge. (The neutrons have no effect either way because they carry no electrical charge.)

Light and Heavy Elements

The number of electrons orbiting the nucleus depends on how many protons exist in that nucleus. Because the two particles cancel out each other's electrical charges, there must be an electron for each proton. The number of electrons usually equals the number of protons. (The number of neutrons in the nucleus often equals the number of protons, but sometimes there are more neutrons than protons.)

The number of protons and electrons also determines the specific type of atom. Each of the basic elements in nature is made up of an atom with a different number of protons in its nucleus. The simplest, lightest element—a gas called "hydrogen"—has a nucleus containing a single proton. As expected, a hydrogen atom has one electron, too. The next heaviest element—helium, another gas—has two protons and two electrons.

As the numbers of protons and electrons increase, the elements their atoms form get heavier and heavier. One of the most important of these elements is carbon. Lots of carbon can

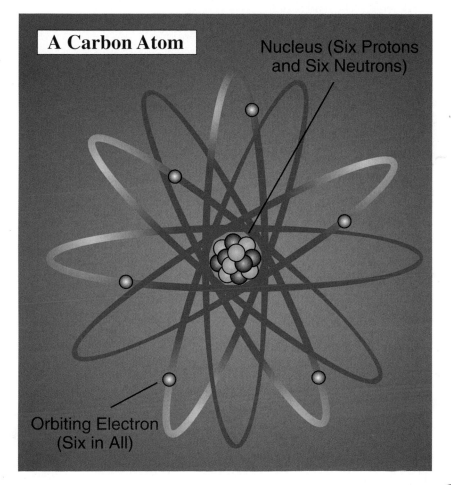

A Carbon Atom

Nucleus (Six Protons and Six Neutrons)

Orbiting Electron (Six in All)

be found in coal and the bodies of animals and people. A carbon atom has six protons and six electrons. The heaviest natural element of all is uranium. It has ninety-two protons in its nucleus and the same number of electrons orbiting the nucleus.

The Subatomic Zoo

Protons, electrons, and neutrons are not the only subatomic particles that exist within the atom. In the twentieth century, scientists discovered a large number of even smaller particles. One of these is the **quark**. Quarks seem to be the building blocks of the heavy particles in an atom's nucleus. Scientists believe that each proton and neutron is made up of two or three quarks.

Another subatomic particle, the neutrino, sometimes goes hand in hand with the electron. Neutrinos also pair themselves with other particles, including muons, which are like heavy electrons. Scientists often call neutrinos "ghostlike," partly because they have very little mass. A neutrino is thousands of times lighter than an electron, which is itself a very light particle. Because they are so small, neutrinos can pass right through most solid objects. Millions of them are whizzing through our bodies right now.

Over two hundred subatomic particles have been discovered so far. They show a wide variety

Some scientists attempt to capture some tiny quarks.

This is a computer image of a molecule. Most known substances are made up of molecules.

of sizes and behaviors. So scientists sometimes jokingly compare them to little animals living in a "subatomic zoo."

Atoms Form Molecules

The atoms that have these microscopic zoos of particles only rarely exist all by themselves. Most of the time, the atoms of the ninety-two natural elements join together to form little groups, or clusters, of atoms. The name for these atomic clusters is "molecules." Nearly every substance in nature is made up of molecules of one sort or another.

One of the simplest and most familiar molecules is that of ordinary water. It has one oxygen atom and two hydrogen atoms. Scientists use a simple formula to describe this combination—H_2O. The H stands for hydrogen; and the little number 2 following it indicates that two hydrogen atoms are in the molecule. The O stands for the single oxygen atom.

Many molecules are a good deal larger and more complex than those of water. A molecule of sugar, for instance, has forty-five atoms. Twelve of these are carbon atoms, twenty-two are hydrogen, and eleven are oxygen. So the formula for sugar is $C_{12}H_{22}O_{11}$. Some molecules are even larger, having hundreds or even thousands of atoms.

Nature has many different kinds and levels of building blocks. Quarks combine to make protons

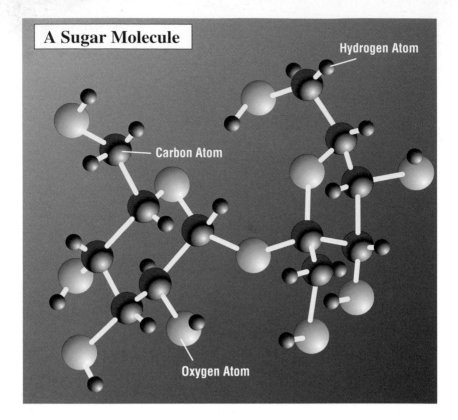

A Sugar Molecule

Hydrogen Atom

Carbon Atom

Oxygen Atom

and neutrons. Then the protons and neutrons join with other particles to make atoms. Finally, various kinds of atoms combine to form molecules, which in turn make up all the things we see and touch, including ourselves. Therefore, the tiny world that exists beyond the limits of our vision is highly complex and truly wondrous.

Chapter 2

Unstable Atoms and Radioactivity

For many years after scientists proved that atoms existed, they assumed these tiny building blocks did not change. In their view, nothing could get into an atom. And none of an atom's energy, including its individual particles, could get out.

This view of atoms turned out to be wrong. Around the beginning of the twentieth century, scientists discovered that some of the energy inside atoms *does* escape sometimes. They named this energy "**radiation**." Radiation can be either subatomic particles or tiny energetic waves. Both are invisible to the eye. And both move at extremely high speeds, hundreds of times faster than a bullet fired by a gun.

Radioactive Decay

Scientists found that radiation can be produced in several different ways. The first way is natural. In other words, some atoms give off radiation all by themselves. This happens partly because all of the protons in an atom's nucleus have positive electrical charges. When two positive charges meet, each pushes the other away. (The same thing happens when two particles with negative charges meet.) In lighter atoms, with only a few protons, this effect is small. So it does not keep the nucleus from holding itself together. Such atoms are said to be stable.

In contrast, the heaviest elements, among them uranium, thorium, and radium, have many protons in their nuclei. The force of their protons is very strong. They are so strong, in fact, that they can sometimes overpower the forces that hold nuclei together. So a few particles in these nuclei fly out and leave the atom, becoming radiation. These atoms are unstable and radioactive.

Because uranium, with ninety-two protons, is the heaviest natural element, it is also the most unstable. So uranium loses some of its protons over time. A uranium atom gives off two protons to try to become more stable. This reduces the number of protons in its nucleus to ninety. But it also changes its nature. The uranium atom

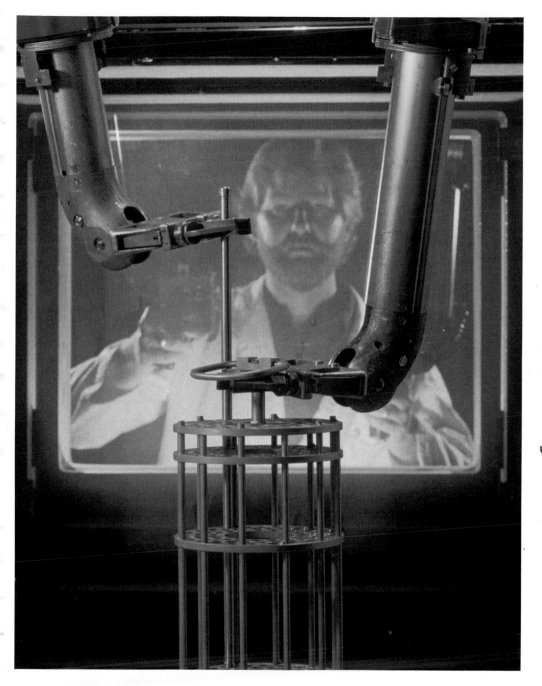

To protect himself from radiation, a researcher uses robotic arms to handle radioactive material.

changes into an atom of thorium, which has a nucleus of ninety protons. This process, in which the atoms of an element try to become more stable by giving off radiation, is called "**radioactive decay**."

Such decay does not end when uranium turns into thorium. Thorium atoms are also unstable. So they, too, give off radiation over time. In fact, all of the elements heavier than lead go through radioactive decay. Atoms of lead, which have eighty-two protons each, are stable. So they do not decay and that is where the process stops.

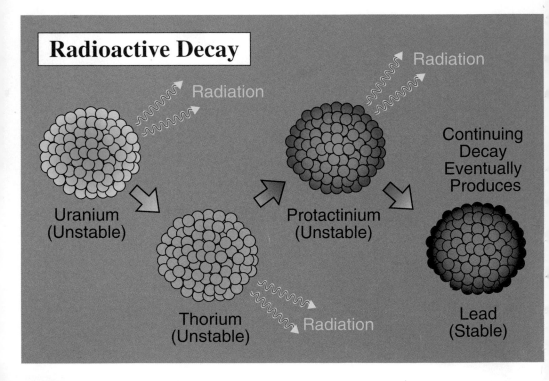

Radioactive Decay

Radiation

Radiation

Uranium (Unstable)

Thorium (Unstable)

Radiation

Protactinium (Unstable)

Continuing Decay Eventually Produces

Lead (Stable)

Atomic Half-Lives

One question scientists ask about these unstable heavy elements is why the planet's original supplies of them have not disappeared by now because of radioactive decay.

Part of the answer to this question is that some of the original supplies of these elements *have* disappeared. For example, protactinium, the second heaviest element (having atoms with ninety-one protons in their nuclei), decayed into lighter elements long ago.

This happened because protactinium has a very short half-life. A radioactive element's half-life is the amount of time it takes one half of that element's atoms to decay. Protactinium's half-life is only a few minutes. So half of a sample of the element will be gone in a few minutes. Half of what is left will decay in another few minutes, and so forth. All of the planet's original protactinium was gone in less than a day. The only reason that tiny traces of protactinium exist on Earth today is that the heavier element, uranium, is constantly decaying. And some uranium atoms turn into protactinium atoms.

On the other hand, Earth still has some of its original uranium because that element has an unusually long half-life. Uranium's half-life is about 4.5 billion years, approximately the age of the planet. This means that roughly half of Earth's

All of the original protactinium on Earth disappeared in less than a day.

original uranium is still around. And it will take another 4.5 billion years for half of what is left to break down into lighter elements.

X Rays

Radioactive decay is only one of the ways that atoms and their subatomic particles produce radiation naturally. Another way is through collisions of atoms and particles. Such collisions often occur when particles are moving at high speeds. When an electrically charged particle, such as an electron, strikes another particle or an atom, the collision creates a tiny burst of radiation. Scientists call this wavelike form of radiation "X rays." Countless subatomic collisions occur all the time in outer space, on the sun, and on Earth. And these events give off X rays.

When scientists discovered and began studying X rays (in the late 1800s), they noticed a peculiar property of this radiation. Namely, X rays can pass right through many solid materials. Among these materials are the flesh and bones that make up the human body. Researchers quickly recognized the potential for using X rays to see inside the body without cutting it open. Taking X-ray pictures of the body reveals the existence of broken bones, tumors, and other problems. After checking a patient's X ray, a doctor can better plan an effective treatment.

Taking a medical X ray of a patient is one of the most common examples of artificial, or human-made, radiation. A modern X-ray machine con-

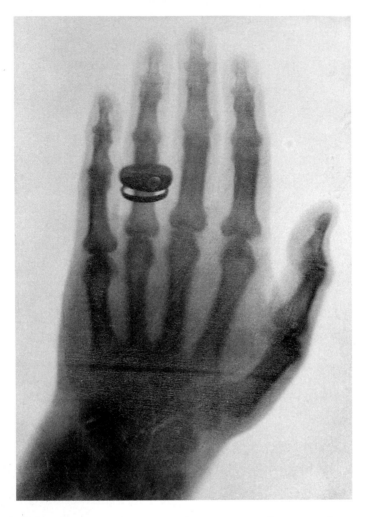

One of the first X rays ever taken was an image of a human hand with a ring on one finger.

sists in part of a glass tube from which the air has been removed. Electricity heats up a substance at one end of the tube, and the atoms of that substance give off electrons. The electrons speed through the tube and strike a piece of metal at the other end. Resulting atomic collisions within the metal produce a burst of X rays. Then the radiation passes through the patient's body and collects on a piece of photographic film. Developing the film reveals a sort of photograph of a patient's insides.

The Need for Caution

People can only be exposed to X rays for short periods of time and infrequently. If too many X rays pass through the body too often, they can damage its cells. Several other kinds of radiation, including those produced by radioactive decay,

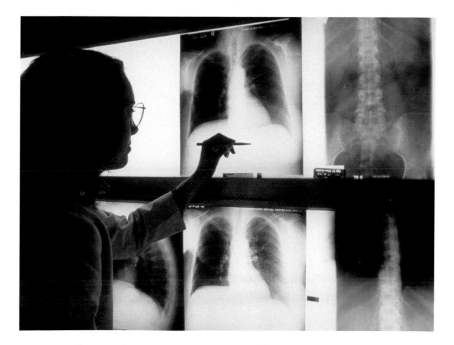

Doctors use X rays such as these to find broken bones, tumors, and other medical problems.

are even more harmful to life. Exposure to large amounts of these kinds of radiation can cause sickness and even death.

So people who constantly work around or handle radioactive materials must be very careful. That is why the technicians who take medical X rays stand behind lead shields. (Lead is very dense and absorbs most radiation.) Workers in nuclear power plants also protect themselves with special radiation-proof shields or clothing.

Chapter 3

Nuclear Power Plants

In the past century or so, scientists learned a great deal about atoms. They proved that atoms are nature's building blocks and showed that they give off radiation. Scientists also discovered that atomic nuclei have a lot of energy locked or stored inside them.

Beginning in the late 1930s, researchers learned to release some of the energy stored in atomic nuclei. They found that they could make powerful weapons. In 1945 scientists exploded the first atom bomb in a desert in New Mexico. Soon afterward the United States dropped two of these bombs on Japan, ending World War II (fought by the United States and its allies against Japan and Germany).

In the years following the war, scientists also tried to find peaceful uses for nuclear energy. In particular, they saw nuclear energy as a new way to meet the world's ever-growing need for electricity.

Trinity, the first atomic bomb ever exploded, lights up the New Mexico desert in 1945.

 Atoms

The first nuclear power plants were built in the 1950s. Today about four hundred such plants exist worldwide and produce almost one-fifth of the world's electricity.

Nuclear Fission

The nuclei of the atoms that make up Earth do not naturally give off enough energy to power whole cities. Scientists must encourage the atoms to release that energy. The process they use to do this is called "**fission**," which comes from a Latin word meaning "to split." Quite literally, fission splits atoms in half.

The atoms of almost any element can be split in half. However, atoms of very heavy elements like uranium and thorium work best for fission. First, they are large, so they have more energy stored inside them than lighter atoms. Second, they are unstable. That makes them easier to break apart.

The most common substance used for fuel in nuclear power plants is an unstable form of uranium called uranium 235. Plant workers aim a small beam of neutrons at a piece of uranium 235. Some of the neutrons strike atoms within the uranium. These atoms split in half, each releasing two or three neutrons of their own, plus a small burst of energy. Some of the neutrons given off by the uranium atoms then strike nearby uranium atoms. These also break in half and release neutrons and energy. As more and more atoms in the fuel split, the process expands and speeds up. Scientists call this a "**chain reaction**." It takes place extremely fast—in less than a second—and releases an enormous amount of energy.

It is not difficult to see what would happen if such a chain reaction was allowed to continue unchecked. All of the atoms in the uranium fuel

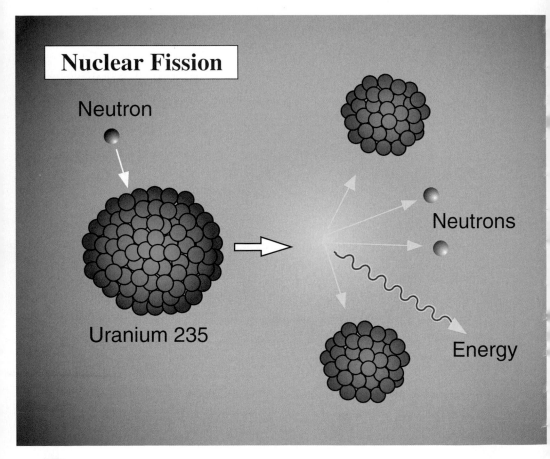

would quickly release their stored energy. And a gigantic burst of heat and light would explode outward in all directions. This, of course, is the principle of the atom bomb. However, in a nuclear power plant, the workers take steps to ensure that this does not happen. They use different methods to keep the chain reaction under control. The result is the creation of a large amount of heat, which they convert into electricity.

An Uncertain Future

The process of making electricity from heat generated by nuclear fission is very efficient. However, it is also very costly. A nuclear power plant requires huge amounts of metal and concrete to shield the workers and the outside world from harmful radiation. It must also be equipped with other safeguards to avoid **meltdowns**. It now costs several billion dollars to build such a plant. In many places, coal- or gas-burning power plants can be built cheaper.

Nuclear power plants can also be dangerous to the soil, water, air, and people around them. Accidents at these plants are rare, but when they occur they can be devastating. In 1986, for example, an explosion occurred in the nuclear plant in Chernobyl, in Ukraine. Large amounts of harmful radiation leaked into the environment, and more than a hundred people died. In addition, years later, many people developed illnesses such as cancer and some babies were born with deformities.

Concerns over costs and safety have made building new nuclear power plants in the United States difficult. Some countries, including Austria, Sweden, and the Philippines, have actually given up on nuclear power. A few others,

Like other nuclear power plants, this one has a large concrete dome to hold in dangerous radiation.

The Chernobyl nuclear power plant in Ukraine was the site of a serious accident that occurred in 1986.

though, are still building such plants. Among them are Russia, Japan, and India. For the moment, therefore, the future of nuclear power is unclear. And for a long time to come, most of the world's electricity will still come from non-nuclear plants.

Chapter 4

Other Modern Uses for Atoms

Making electricity continues to be one of the major ways that people use atoms. But nuclear plants that produce power through fission have raised concerns about high costs and safety. So scientists are trying to find a cheaper, safer way to produce power with atoms. Many experts predict that such a method will be perfected some time in this century.

In the meantime, scientists have found numerous other practical ways to use atoms. One of these is telling time. A device called an "atomic clock" keeps time far more accurately than standard mechanical clocks and watches. Scientists also use atoms in medicine. Most of these involve methods of seeing inside the body to detect disease or other problems. Using X rays to take pictures of bones and other internal body parts is just one example.

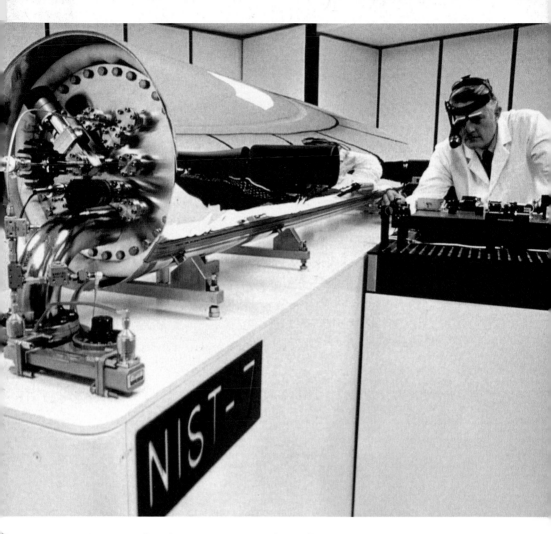

A scientist checks an atomic clock for accuracy.

X Rays in Three Dimensions

Another method doctors use to create images of the inside of the body is called a **CAT scan**. The three letters stand for "computerized axial tomography." A CAT scan is more advanced than an

X ray. An X ray is a two-dimensional picture, while a CAT scan is a three-dimensional picture.

A CAT-scan machine has a large, doughnut-shaped scanner. The scanner surrounds the head, leg, or other body part the doctor wants to image. A standard X-ray machine takes a picture from only one direction; the CAT scanner snaps pictures from many different directions at the same time. The scanner is connected to a computer. The computer collects the various pictures taken by the scanner and combines them into one three-dimensional image. The doctor then examines this image on a screen.

CAT scans are used to examine many parts of the body. But they are especially useful for studying the brain. A CAT scan reveals brain tumors and areas of the brain damaged by stroke (sudden loss of blood flow to the brain). This technique is also good at measuring the thickness of bone tissue.

Watching the Organs Move

Another method that uses radiation is called a "**PET scan**." The three letters stand for "positron-emission tomography." Unlike X rays and CAT scans, a PET scan does not work by passing radiation *through* the body. Instead, a PET scan detects and takes pictures of radiation *given off* by the body.

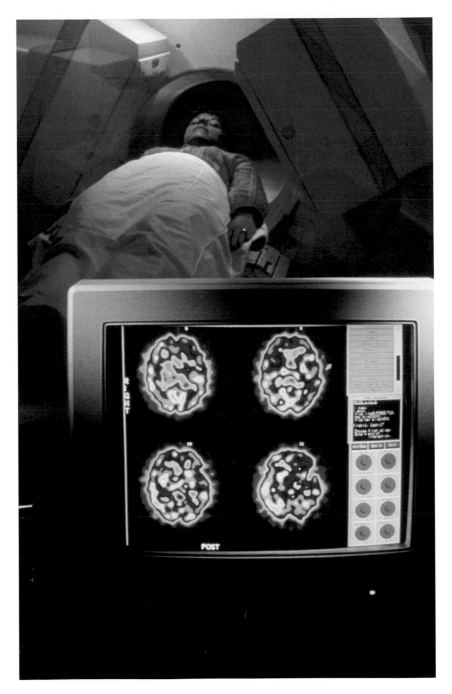

A monitor displays images of the brain of the patient seen undergoing a CAT scan.

The PET scanner is designed to detect a subatomic particle called a "positron." This is a peculiar kind of electron that has a positive rather than a negative charge. Using a needle, a doctor or nurse injects the patient with a substance that gives off positrons. The patient then lies down for one to two hours. During that time, the substance travels through the bloodstream, reaching the heart and other organs. The PET scanner can "see" the positrons; and it takes pictures of one or more organs from various angles. As in the case of a CAT scanner, the PET scanner is hooked up to a computer, which produces color images on a screen.

PET scans have one advantage over X rays and CAT scans. The latter two methods take still pictures of an organ. These pictures may not show any tumors, injuries, or other problems with the organ; but the patient may insist that he or she feels discomfort or pain in the area. A PET scan can see an organ in motion as the blood moves through it. This enables the doctor to tell if that organ is actually working properly and perhaps pinpoint the problem. PET scans are particularly useful for studying blood flow in the heart.

Atomic Timekeeping

While PET scanners rely on detecting positrons, atomic clocks detect movements made by more

A PET scan can see a person's insides in motion, often helping doctors pinpoint a problem.

standard electrons (i.e., those having negative electrical charges). In principle, the electrons used in such clocks can be from atoms of any substance. However, scientists have found that atoms of cesium work best. (Each cesium atom has fifty-five protons and the same number of electrons.) Cesium atomic clocks are so accurate that they have an error of less than one second every 300,000 years!

A cesium atomic clock consists of a small chamber in which the operator puts a tiny bit of cesium. He or she then aims a gentle beam of wavelike radiation at the sample. The radiation causes the electrons in the cesium atoms to spin in a slightly different manner. Only radiation with waves of a certain size and number per second can make this happen. Moreover, their size and number are always precisely the same.

Scientists take a measurement of these waves and call it an "atomic second." An atomic second is very short; a normal second (1/60 of a minute) consists of millions of them. Computers convert the number of atomic seconds into normal seconds, minutes, and hours. In 1967 countries around the world signed an agreement to base their official timekeeping on the atomic second of the cesium atom. Other kinds of atomic clocks are also in use. But the cesium version remains the standard.

The Power That Drives the Stars

Atomic clocks, X-ray machines, PET scanners, and other devices that work with atoms and sub-atomic particles are obviously useful. They serve humanity by improving efficiency or the quality of life. Other important atom-based tools are yet to come.

The most promising of all are small power plants that will work by nuclear **fusion**. In a way, fusion is the opposite of fission. While fission splits atoms in half, fusion, which is much more powerful, *fuses*, or forces atoms together. This is the process that powers the sun and other stars. Inside the sun, extreme heat and pressure force hydrogen atoms together. They fuse to become heavier helium atoms, in the process releasing vast amounts of energy in the form of heat and light.

A number of scientists in various countries are trying to find a way to imitate this process safely on a smaller scale. When they succeed (and there is little doubt they eventually will), the world will be changed. A fusion generator would need only a few ounces of matter to power a home for a year. That matter could be in almost any form. Even garbage can be turned into useable energy. Factories, office buildings, cars, airplanes, boats, spaceships, and more—all will run cheaply on

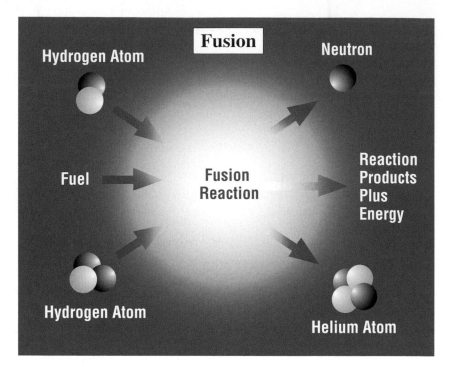

fusion power. They will also run safely because fusion does not produce harmful radiation, as fission does.

In addition to fusion power, scientists will no doubt discover and develop other ways to use atoms. Clearly, humanity has only begun to tap the amazing resources of nature's tiny building blocks.

Glossary

CAT scan: A machine called a scanner takes X-ray pictures of the inside of the body. A computer combines these pictures into a three-dimensional image.

chain reaction: Atoms undergoing fission cause neighboring atoms to split, which in turn cause still other ones to split, and so forth, releasing a large amount of energy in the process.

electron: A subatomic particle that carries a negative electrical charge and orbits an atom's nucleus.

fission: High-speed subatomic particles crash into an atom's nucleus, splitting it in half and releasing energy.

fusion: When extreme heat and pressure force two or more atoms together, creating a heavier atom and releasing energy.

meltdown: In a nuclear power plant, a possible disaster in which the casings of the fuel rods melt and release the radioactive fuel into the environment.

neutron: A subatomic particle that has no electrical charge and is located in an atom's nucleus.

nucleus: The central portion of an atom, where the protons and neutrons are located.

PET scan: A scanner that detects radiation coming from a liquid that has been injected into a patient's body. The scanner uses that radiation to make images of the inside of the body, and a computer processes these images and displays them on a screen.

proton: A subatomic particle that carries a positive electrical charge and is located in an atom's nucleus.

quark: A subatomic particle that scientists believe is a building block of protons and neutrons. In theory, each proton and neutron is made up of two or three quarks.

radiation: Subatomic particles or wavelike energy given off by atoms. Some kinds of radiation are harmful to living things, while other kinds are not.

radioactive decay: When heavy, unstable atoms, such as those of uranium, give off radiation and eventually transform into lighter atoms.

subatomic: Smaller than an atom. The particles that make up an atom are said to be subatomic.

For Further Exploration

Christopher Cooper, *Matter.* New York: Dorling Kindersley, 1992. A big, well-illustrated book that tells what matter is, then explains atoms, molecules, solids, liquids, gases, and other related items.

Ray A. Gallant, *The Ever-Changing Atom.* Tarrytown, NY: Benchmark Books, 2000. This well-written book introduces young readers to the history of the discovery of atoms, from the days of the ancient Greeks to the modern world.

Anne L. Galperin, *Nuclear Energy, Nuclear Waste.* New York: Chelsea House, 1992. Tells about how countries like the United States make nuclear energy in power plants, and also how getting rid of the wastes these plants produce is sometimes a problem. The reading level is junior high school.

Gini Holland, *Nuclear Energy.* Tarrytown, NY: Benchmark Books, 1996. A nicely illustrated introduction to the various ways that humans have learned to tap the energy of the atom.

Carol K. McClafferty, *The Head Bone's Connected to the Neck Bone: The Weird, Wacky and Wonderful X-Ray.* New York: Farrar, Straus and Giroux, 2001. Tells what X rays are and how they help doctors see inside the body.

Don Nardo, *Chernobyl.* San Diego: Lucent Books, 1990. The story of a nuclear power plant in Ukraine that suffered a disaster and caused many people to die of radiation sickness.

Robert E. Wells, *What's Smaller than a Pygmy Shrew?* Morton Grove, IL: Albert Whitman, 1995. Wells begins with the smallest known mammal, then discusses smaller and smaller creatures and things until he reaches the microscopic world of atoms. Highly recommended for young readers.

Charlotte Wilcox, *Powerhouse: Inside a Nuclear Power Plant.* Minneapolis: Carolrhoda Books, 1996. A worthwhile introduction to how a nuclear power plant works.

Index

atom bombs, 25, 29
atomic clocks, 32, 36, 38
atomic seconds, 38
atoms
   size of, 6
   stable, 16
Austria, 30

cancer, 30
carbon, 9–10
CAT (computerized axial
   tomography) scans,
   33–34, 36
cesium, 38
chain reactions, 28–29
Chernobyl, 29–30

electrical charges, 8
electrons
   in atomic clocks, 38
   electrical charge of, 8,
     36
   number of, 8–10
   orbits of, 6–8
   X rays and, 22–23
elements, 8–10, 19
energy waves, 15

fission, 27
fusion, 39

gases, 8–9
Greeks, 4

half-lives, 19
helium, 9
hydrogen, 8–9, 13

illness, 30
India, 31

Japan, 25, 31

lead, 18
lead shields, 24

matter, 4–5
medicine
   CAT scans and, 33–34, 36
   PET scans and, 34, 36
   X rays and, 21–23, 32–34,
     36
meltdowns, 29
molecules, 13
muons, 10

neutrinos, 10
neutrons, 6–8
   quarks and, 13–14
   in uranium 235, 27–28
nuclear fission, 27

Picture Credits

In addition to his acclaimed volumes on ancient civilizations, historian Don Nardo has published several studies of modern scientific discoveries and phenomena. Among these are *The Extinction of the Dinosaurs, Vaccines,* and a biography of Charles Darwin, who advanced the modern theory of evolution. Mr. Nardo lives with his wife, Christine, in Massachusetts.